Randolph

DISCARDED BY
MEMPHIS PUBLIC LIBRARY

FIGHTING THE GIANT

From the railyards of Tennessee

all the way to the Supreme Court

by Sheila White

Fighting the Giant

© Copyright 2007 by Sheila White

ISBN: 978-0-9798633-3-2

This book is based on a true story.
The names have been changed to protect the innocent.

All rights reserved under International and Pan-American copyright conventions. No part of this publication may be reproduced, stored in a retrieval system or transmitted in any form or by any means, electronic, mechanical, photocopies, recording or otherwise, without the prior written consent of the author.

To order additional books, go to:
www.RP-Author.com/SWhite

First Edition: 2007

Printed in the United States of America

Robertson Publishing
59 N. Santa Cruz Avenue, Suite B
Los Gatos, California 95030 USA
(888) 354-5957 • www.RobertsonPublishing.com

Table of Contents

Dedication i
Foreword iii
Participants v

The Beginning 1
Documentation Time 7
End of the Probation 11
My Foreman Returns 13
Racial Tensions 19
My Ordeal After Filing Charges 25
My State of Mind 33
Return to Work 35
The Countdown 47
Saving Myself, the Railroad, and Everyone Else 53

Special Thanks 59
Commentary 60
Resources 61

DEDICATION

To my children, Patrice, Monica, and Jonathan, and my parents, family, and friends.

It is my hope that this book will be an inspiration to all people who are working under difficult circumstances.

FOREWORD

I was born in Memphis, Tennessee and attended neighborhood schools which were never integrated. My high school years were filled with the civil rights issues and I became very interested in the activities of Dr. Martin Luther King and Black History. I wanted to go to "war" to create change, but my parents preached the non-violence approach. While I had completed high school with some specific job skills, my marriage and children dictated a need for a higher level of income. I found factory work but I never lost my interest in wanting to see changes in the way people should be treated - as equals and as human beings.

I started working at the Burlington Northern and Santa Fe Railroad as a forklift operator in 1997, because it was my understanding that this company wanted to employ female workers in certain positions. My interview was conducted by two people: Will, the foreman, and Jill of management personnel in Chicago, Illinois. I met all of the qualifications for the forklift position and was hired. Earnings through this type of employment would allow me, as a single parent, to support my three children adequately.

I just wanted to do my work and receive fair and equitable treatment. I had worked in companies before where men and women did the same kind of work and usually helped each other when difficult situations occurred. I knew that women worked at various jobs with the railroad companies before starting my job with Burlington Northern.

On my very first day of work at Burlington Northern I was told repeatedly by many of the male workers that I was not welcome and that I needed to find another job because the railroad was no place for women. I had no idea that I would experience a situation that would require me to file charges against my employer for sexual harassment, retaliation, and discrimination. Over a period of many years I was degraded as a person and stripped of respect. My pride as a person of worth was damaged, but I decided to stand strong and firm and go to war. My anger turned into fighting power. This feeling of empowerment led me to seek the advice of Attorney Donald Donati. He and his team of attorneys helped to see that justice would be served.

It took nine years for these charges of sexual harassment, retaliation, and discrimination to travel from the railroad yards in Memphis all the way to the Supreme Court of the United States, but I stuck it out. It took persistence, commitment, and courage to follow this through to it's final conclusion.

I came to realize that this action would have far-reaching results that would overshadow my own difficulties; I was thrilled that the Court's decision would touch so many people. My lawsuit against the Burlington Northern and Sante Fe Railroad changed the laws of the United States of America. Not only could they not push me around, they can't push you around either. Not anymore.

PARTICIPANTS

Attorneys .... Adair, Evins, Michaels

Burlington Northern
and Santa Fe Railroad .... The Company

Driver .... Jack

Foremen .... Andrew, Carson, Carter, Eddie, Jason, Mark, Nathan, Nick, Paul, Sue, Will

Forklift Operators .... Ben, Sheila

Management Personnel .... Jill, Jim

Physicians .... Grant, West

Superintendent .... Collins

Supervisors .... Alex, Barry, Carl, Gary, Larry

Therapists .... Lindsey, Olds

Trackmen/Track Persons ..... Bob, Dan, Jeff, Jerry, Martin, Matt, Rose, Sally, Sheila, Smith, Ted, Tom

Union Representative .... Bill

The Beginning

On June 23, 1997 Burlington Northern and Sante Fe Railway hired seven people to work in the Tennessee yards in Memphis. These were six men: Bob, Dan, Ted, Ross, Jerry and Martin, and me - Sheila White, all assigned to work in the Maintenance of Way Department. We would be working for the second largest railroad company in the United States (Hoover's Profile, 2007).

The very first day we met our foreman, Will, who seemed to be in his sixties. He was a stocky man of 5'4" with thin hair who loved to chew tobacco. He held a meeting with us outside the tool house on a hot and humid day. As we stood there in the sun, he told us about our new jobs. He called us by our given names, which I learned was the practice used by all people in the yards. He said one would be a truck driver; five would be trackmen and work on the railroad tracks, and I would be a forklift operator. Will went over the safety rules and what we would do in our jobs. He issued us hard hats, safety glasses, ear plugs, and gloves. He said that weather for the most part would not affect the kind of work the trackmen had to do. He also told us that we would be on call at night for any emergencies such as derailments and track problems.

Will said that he would keep records of our work hours, including overtime and derailment call-outs and would submit this information in time for the biweekly payroll schedule. There was no time clock; our standard work hours were from 7:30 A.M. to 3:30 P.M. We were told that when a work assignment went beyond the 3:30 P.M. quitting time, we had to remain on the job until it was completed. We were expected to report to our work shift the next morning at 7:30 A.M. This was also the requirement when we worked on derailments.

In this briefing on the first day with all seven of us, Will said loudly, "Hey, Sheila, when you come on your period, let me know." All of the men in the group looked at me in a strange way. Some shook their heads because nobody could believe he had made that statement. I was speechless and humiliated. Oh, what a first day! I had never heard of a person in a supervisory position bring up such a personal matter in front of others.

This same day a male co-worker let me know that I had to pull my load and that I was not to ask for help. He also reminded me that I was the only female among the 50 to 70 men in the Maintenance of Way Department. I found that I would face open resentment for being a female in a male oriented work environment. Despite this, I was very excited to start my new job. I now had a good salary, enabling me to take care of my family. I listened, observed, and tried to take everything in stride.

My first day as a forklift operator started my ninety day probationary period. I replaced Ben who had been operating the forklift at the time I was hired. He had been a trackman originally, a senior position that paid more. While operating the forklift, he received a "per diem" which kept his salary at the same level.

As forklift operator for this department, my job activity included receiving and unloading supplies from semi-trailer trucks, logging in supplies and materials, placing them in their specific areas in the tool house, calling the departments in the yards to pick up their orders and getting ready the supply orders that the foremen made for the next working day. I found it necessary to keep a record for myself of what was received and what was distributed. I kept the work area, inside and outside, clean and free of clutter. A note pad became part of my equipment.

Beginning with my second day in the yards I realized that I was more or less on display. I noticed that the workers were bringing their wives to work in order to see "that woman" who had been hired to work with their spouses.

Each morning at the briefings during the last week in June 1997 my foreman, Will, began to make specific references to me as a female. In July 1997 I began to jot down dates, the names of people working around me, and comments that were made throughout the day about my work activity and about me. Some comments were positive. Others were negative and sexist in nature. Each morning a few men joked about my carrying a note pad and asked if I was the "tool house lawyer". We laughed, but they did not really understand what I was doing or how extensive my note taking had become. At that time I did not know that I would one day have to use the notes that I made about each work day activity. These notes became a daily journal.

There were many nights when we had call-outs for train derailments. The procedure involved the foreman calling track persons to see if they were available to work derailment. If the person was not available to take the call, the foreman would leave a message for the track person to call him. I returned calls to my foreman's home on several occasions. He or his wife would then call me back and give me the location.

Now derailment or repair work at night had to be done in all kinds of weather — rain, sleet, snow, cold and below freezing, or hot and humid. It did not matter because the work had to be done so that the trains could move. In the locations where we worked at night, it was usually "pitch dark" and the only lights we had were those we provided — for ourselves. The stillness of the night was broken by piercing noises. These came from trucks used to provide power to hydraulic lines for jack hammers, spikers, and drill machines; rails clanging as they hit each other; and loud voices yelling instructions and calling for tools and supplies. The tools and equipment were on trucks and had to be taken off in order to be used. Now there was no tool or piece of equipment that weighed less than 50 pounds. I was assigned to a supply truck with the duty of getting workers what they needed off the truck. When I could not pick up, toss, or maneuver the heavier equipment from the truck, I would ask certain track persons to help me. They never refused my request. At all times the air was filled with dust that came from the work we were doing. This night call-out work had no specific number of hours. It was over when it was over – meaning when the derailment was cleared.

Early one morning at work, Will said to me: "Some white folks don't like Blacks calling their house." I looked at him and said, "I called your house because you left a message and wanted to know if I was available to work the derailment. I needed to get the location of the derailment." This was a wake-up call. The procedure for me would be different. I was not to call his house for any reason. He did not give me the name of another person or a different number to call. Pressure was building in me because of the remarks Will, my foreman, constantly made about my sex and my working in this job, but I managed to appear calm and cool on the outside.

On another occasion he asked my thoughts about a white man going out with black women. Now, I was still on probation. I had to be careful about what I said and how I said it; I did not need to incite more complaints. Still, some male workers complained that this forklift job should belong to a worker with more seniority. Yet no worker had bid on it. Therefore the job was open for a new hire.

Every morning before I went to work, I prayed for strength to get through the day. I had to be mindful of any activity that would set me up to be terminated or fired. Over and over I was being told by the very foreman who had hired me that I needed to find another job because the railroad was not a place for me. I told him, "I need to work and make a living just like you." I also told him he could stop saying that because he was wasting his breath. Other remarks of a harassing nature were made by my foreman every day and at times by some co-workers, such as I could get fired and I could get hurt while working. I tried not to think about these comments, but they were being made too frequently for me to overlook.

Documentation Time

I had the feeling that something was about to happen that could jeopardize my job at the Tennessee yards. My note taking became more important, and I started documenting all incidents that involved my co-workers and me. I kept a journal about the time, dates, and places where incidents occurred and the persons involved in the matter. At times I did this toward the end of the work day. When I could not write this material down around that time, I recounted the events of the day when I got home and entered the incidents in my journal.

My probationary period was nearly up. I was reminded frequently by some co-workers that the superintendent and the supervisor wanted my foreman to "disqualify" me before the end of my probationary period. It was a known but unspoken feeling that some people in higher positions in the yards resented being required by law to hire a woman for this department. At the same time my foreman Will had to put down that I came to work on time and did what I was asked to do. He also had to admit that I was a good worker and that I worked better at my job than some of the men who had been there for a long time, which was at complete odds with his attitude and behavior towards me.

One night in late September 1997 we were called to work on a train derailment. I was the second person to arrive around 11:00 P.M. at the location, and we were waiting for our foreman, Will to show up. I heard someone call my name. I turned around and saw that Will, my foreman, was calling to me. He had arrived late at the job site and was wearing street clothing – pants, shirt, and cowboy boots. He yelled for me to come where he was. Since it was very dark in the area where we were, I had to use my flashlight.

When I got to where he was, he said, "Hey, Sheila, shine the light on me while I pee." I told my foreman, who smelled of alcohol, never to do that to me again. Another foreman heard him and immediately left the scene without saying or doing anything. He knew that this was wrong and didn't want to be part of the situation. I documented the incident. The next morning other workers, all male, began complaining about the incident when we reported for work. The discussions between groups of workers were becoming heated. Some members of my work group were very concerned and upset while others didn't seem to care. Shortly thereafter all of the employees in the yards heard the story. I was asked by Collin, the superintendent, if this incident really did occur. I asked for a conference, which was set for that afternoon.

In this conference with Superintendent Collin and my supervisor Larry, I told them what had happened that night and also of the problem I was having with my foreman and some male co-workers. They laughed and said they would look into the matter. Immediately after I left their office and returned to the tool house, some of my co-workers told me about what had taken place in my meeting with my superiors. They also knew about the contact that had been made with headquarters (Chicago, Illinois and Fort Worth, Texas) to alert them about my concerns.

The in-house investigation began with Jim, the manager in Memphis. He interviewed all of the men in my department to determine if my complaints were true. Later Jill, who I had originally interviewed with for the job, came all the way from the Chicago office to ask more questions. Some workers said they did not see anything being done to me. A number of co-workers had witnessed the incidents and they did not change their reports. They said Jill grilled them repeatedly and seemed dissatisfied with the way they continued to respond to her questions. They felt she had a bad attitude.

What was I feeling at this point? I was glad that these co-workers and some foremen had responded truthfully and they did not allow anyone to get them to change their statements about the kind of treatment I was receiving from my foreman.

I also had to deal with the group of co-workers who openly told me that I should have kept my mouth closed. They told me that I was attacking an employee with 30 years of service who would be believed over me, a worker just completing her probationary period. These people did not know me. I told the workers that a new day had come. I would not allow this kind of action on my job to continue to happen to me. That day I decided to stand "tall" and not give in, no matter what else could or would happen. I had "fire power" within me.

The in-house investigation took three days. At the end of the third day, I was called to the office of Superintendent Collin, along with Larry, my supervisor on September 26, 1997. They told me that the investigation had been completed. Several decisions had been made which they wanted to share with me. My foreman, Will, would receive a ten day suspension and would have to attend a sexual harassment classes.

The second part of the decision was that my job was no longer that of a forklift operator. I was being assigned to work on the tracks with the men. I would report the next day to a work gang. I looked at both of them with tears in my eyes. I tried to keep my self-control although I was both angry and confused over their decision. I told them that they were punishing me for reporting incidents of harassment and they were wrong. I stormed out of the office.

Perhaps providentially as I was leaving the conference site in the Main Building, I overheard a conversation between a supervisor and Will. The supervisor was telling Will to get rid of me before I completed my probationary period. I knew I had to be careful, do my work and be on guard.

Did I get my job as forklift operator back? NO! The same man who gave it up in June 1997 when I started to work in the Tennessee yards took the job again. Will was suspended. I had to wait until the next day to find out more about my new job duties from my new foreman, Carter.

End Of Probation

For ten work days while Will was out on suspended leave, I was part of a work gang with Carter, a foreman who looked after the work needs of his group. I learned what kind of work trackmen or track persons had to do. The work included repairing railroad tracks and broken rails, loading and unloading rails and ties, spiking, loading and unloading spikes, pulling spikes with a spike puller, loading and setting plates, using claw bar and hydraulic tools, oiling and adjusting switches, pulling line connectors for machines or tools, loading spike cans (barrels) for gangs, and knocking anchors on or off.

The track persons worked eight hours a day doing this type of labor as rail gangs and switch gangs. Track persons assigned to the Tennessee yards worked on The Company's rail lines going through Memphis and at times on locations such as Marion and Wilson, Arkansas, Hamilton, Birmingham, Demopolis and Guin in Alabama and Cape Girardeau, Missouri.

My probationary period ended in October 1997. Officially I was a "railroader" and I joined the union, Brotherhood of Maintenance of Way. I continued to do my job as track person each day. The work atmosphere was still tense. Workers looked at me and questioned whether I could handle the job or workload. Some began to speculate on when I was going to quit. Some workers set a fast pace and complained that I was not able to keep up with the assignment. I was new, learning to do my job *on* the job — on assignments with experienced workers. They knew shortcuts and had techniques that I would have to learn to become more skilled. There were some workers who more or less guided me and helped me. They slowed the work pace just a little so that I could do the job correctly. I learned how to develop techniques that would help me, a left-handed person who was working with right-handed people. I knew that I would persevere on this job, no matter what happened.

I remembered that as a child I had been ambidextrous. I will never forget my aunt Edith Pearl, who was left-handed, which most people didn't know. Aunt Edith had learned how to use her right hand to do a lot of things except write. I watched her in action and learned many of her techniques.

My Foreman Returns

When his ten day suspension was up, Will returned to work. He announced to some workers in my presence that he enjoyed those days off because he received his vacation pay and he did not attend any kind of "sex" classes. All he had to do was to sign some papers. He said that The Company had to say something about this suspension and sexual harassment classes for the record. I just looked at him and I kept my anger in check. My supervisor, Larry, moved me from Carter's work gang and placed me once again under Will's supervision.

Will began to show a vindictive side. It seemed that he was getting pressure from some higher-ups to get me out of the way. Several times he said I had embarrassed him and The Company. Some workers had asked him how he could let a black woman bring him down like that. Two co-workers expressed their belief that some of the men had caused problems between Will and me. One indicated that he and others could do something bad to me.

I went to both, stood as tall as my slender 5'1" frame would let me and told them to "shut the hell up", as this matter was none of their business and also, "when I pulled their chain, they could bark." That same day they went to Carl, the supervisor on the job site, and told him what I had said. I was called by Carl to come down the hill where he was. He told me that Jeff and Matt said that I was making some allegations against them. I told Carl that I was there when all of the statements were made and he was not there. I knew what I said and they were correct when they stated that I told them that this matter was not their business. I left Carl, the supervisor and went back to work.

At this point I had taken all I could from anyone about this matter or about me as a female worker with the railroad. I began to fight back in ways that did not jeopardize my job. I made every effort to follow the rules while the ones after me broke them.

Will gave me many different duties on job sites. I pulled spike barrels weighing about 100 pounds from the supply truck or railcar. I walked miles along the rails to unload white rock, called chert, from boxcars. The white dust covered me from head to foot and I had no mask to keep me from inhaling it. This dust often got into my mouth, and it was gritty, like sand. I turned cross ties by hand because Will would not allow me to use the proper tools. Although I used gloves, the creosote residue got on my clothing and sometimes on my skin. The odor was strong and it got in my hair and clothing. My eyes burned and I got skin rashes from repeated contact even though I tried to be cautious. If I had been allowed to use the proper tools, all of this would have been minimized.

All of these job assignments carried potential risks that I wasn't aware of at the time. Handling heavy spike barrels repeatedly could injure my wrists and hands and cause carpal tunnel syndrome. The inhaling of the white chert dust could lead to lung problems. Creosote could enter my body through my skin, lungs, and mouth, and cause many serious or even life-threatening problems, including cancer, listed as an occupational disease for railroad workers.

There were other jobs I had to do in the yards and on other job sites where I was not given additional help. My supervisor sometimes did these jobs himself, but always with help. He ordered my gang not to help me. Some employees in the yards told me they were concerned about what The Company was doing, and they cared about my well-being. Through the grapevine in the yards I was sometimes able to pick-up useful information on what was being planned to make my job harder, but Will did not know that I was being forewarned.

More problems, in addition to my changed work assignment, seemed to pop up everywhere I turned. I had to deal on a daily basis with a poor restroom facility, signs of discrimination, and continued harassment. In other departments in the Tennessee yards, separate restroom facilities were available for the male and female workers — but not where I worked. In our tool house the men and I had to share the one and only restroom. I was advised that this was the way we had to deal with this situation. Now, the restroom had two doors – one inside and one that led to the outside of the building. When in use, both doors needed to be locked, but the locks were broken. The men had been accustomed to entering the tool house through this door to the restroom facility. The restroom was always dirty and the odor of urine was very strong. There was no janitorial service. I spoke to the management officers about this situation because the men did not check to see if the restroom was in use. They just barged in. Their attitude was that "that woman" did not need to be in this job.

I was told to put up a sign to indicate the restroom was in use. In this way the men would have to enter the tool house through the front entrance. This did not work all of the time because the locks on the doors were broken. Women who came to this department were not comfortable using this restroom. They had to go to the main building which was a 10 to 12 minute distance by car or a 30 minute walk, depending on car and train traffic.

No provision was ever made for a restroom facility called a 'johnny' for us at the jobs on locations outside the yards. We went into the bushes, tall weeds, or a thicket. I trained myself to eat and drink less. If we were near a business, we could ask to use their restroom, and whenever I was near a facility I forced myself to use it, whether I needed to or not.

There were times when we were a long distance from a town and I needed to use a restroom. I had to get permission to use the truck to go into town. I had to walk to the location where our truck was parked, then I would drive five to ten miles to the town. Sometimes I would be denied the use of a public restroom and had to search for one that I could use. Just imagine how uncomfortable this process was and how I could not control 'Mother Nature' when the urge to relieve myself occurred. I would drive back to the job site parking area, leave the truck, and walk two or more miles back to the job site.

Now the incident about raincoats! The weather forecast was for rain for a number of days, including one where we would be outside all day. Will, our foreman bought raincoats for all of the men in the work gang to have for the next rainy day. I asked him about one for me. He said that he did not see the need for me to have one. I reminded him that I worked in rainy weather also. He did not get one for me. I had to wear my own coat.

At a briefing the next day several work gangs were assembled together. The weather was bad, with a heavy rain.

They had on rainwear and I had on my own coat. Nick, the foreman for the second gang, asked me in everyone's presence: "Where is your raincoat?" I told him Will had said I did not need one. Nick said loudly and emphatically in an authoritative voice, "Will, there will be no work until you buy her a raincoat!" You could hear the men gasp because of the way he addressed Will.

Racial Tensions

There were many work gangs in our department. Working relationships varied according to the makeup of the work gangs. One gang of black workers was headed by a black foreman. Working relations within this gang were essentially cordial and the workers got along with each other. Several gangs of white workers had white foremen. Their working conditions and relationships with each other were good. One gang was interracial and was headed by a white foreman. The working conditions and relationships in this group were altogether different from the others because tensions would flair up when inflammatory statements were made.

One morning six of us were sitting in the tool house where all meetings and briefings took place, waiting to receive our orders for the day. One of the workers in one of the groups remarked several times that President Lincoln should have allowed slavery to continue for a while longer. I was sitting at another table and was writing in my journal. I listened to his remarks but made no comment. Suddenly the room got very quiet and this worker seemed very nervous and tense. The atmosphere throughout the day was tense and everybody moved about cautiously. This worker subsequently left, and obtained employment at a different railroad.

Another incident occurred in Marion, Arkansas while we were on lunch break. Some workers went to a fast food place while we stayed in the tool house. The foreman got an emergency call to come to the fast food place because there had been an accident. Tom, a white worker, liked to keep racial tensions going with his talk. He got caught in his own trap. He told Smith, one of the black workers, that he was glad Dr. King was dead because he kept a lot of mess going on for Blacks. Smith asked him to drop that conversation. Instead, Tom called Smith the "N" word. Smith told Tom not to use that word again. Tom called him the "N" word again. Tom was found on the floor knocked out. That punch was heard all the way from Arkansas to Tennessee.

The Company was upset and embarrassed over the racial tension that had exploded and exposed their need to have sensitivity training for workers. Management had never openly disciplined workers who had expressed their dislike and contempt for certain groups of people.

The action The Company wanted to take in this matter was to fire both workers. Many workers expressed their concern about the severity of this action, especially when Smith did not initiate the incident. Smith was allowed to return many months later, but Tom returned to work shortly after the incident. He never stopped expressing his inflammatory views and belittling people he didn't care for. He also continued the name calling, as did many of the workers in his gang.

I was one of the people Tom didn't care for. He began making remarks about my way of working. He said one thing in particular: "Sheila, you need to pick up the pace. You are holding your tool in the wrong hand." At this point I interrupted Tom's tirade. I said, "I am left handed. I work differently from right-handed people and I might look different while holding my tools. As long as I get the job done, you should keep quiet."

On location in small towns in Arkansas such as Marie, Turrell, Dyess, Joiner, and Marion, sometimes all of the workers would go out to eat on lunch break. We learned the areas where the black workers were not really wanted as customers. The owners of these places would not let us use the restroom facility nor eat in their store. They had no other place for us to wash our hands.

One of the places in particular where black workers experienced this kind of treatment was located in Wilson, Arkansas, a small town of about 900 people. The railroad line runs through the town. The two nearest large cities were Memphis, Tennessee, about 29 miles away and Little Rock, Arkansas, about 139 miles away. There was one particular grocery store in Wilson where the white workers liked to buy food for their lunch. They could get sandwiches or the hot lunches. These workers would place their food orders and then go to the restroom to wash their hands.

As I was about to get my food order, I asked about the restroom. The two cashiers looked at each other and one said that they did not have one. I said very politely that there were federal and state laws that required all places serving food to have public restrooms. I did not buy any food. Instead I went outside to the truck and asked a co-worker to go to the restroom area. He had been to this store many times before and knew where the restroom was. He went inside and walked to the restroom area while I watched from the door. After he returned to the truck, I went back inside. I told the cashiers that my co-worker had been able to use their restroom. One of them replied, "He was not supposed to use the restroom. Now get out of my store!" The white male workers were able to use the restroom facility but the black male workers and I were told the restroom facility was not available to us.

After we had gone through this experience several times, we told Jack, our driver, to let us out at a certain stop. He could pick us up there for our return to the tool house or the work site. We usually found a place where we could have access to a restroom, sit and eat, and be accepted as human beings. I wondered why this kind of activity was still taking place in the twenty-first century.

This brought to mind some things I had read about the railroad and the labor of trackmen. Almost all rail lines built east of the Mississippi River and south of the Mason-Dixon Line before the Civil War used slave labor. Some slaves were bought by the railroad companies and others were obtained through lease or contract from their slave holders. These men generally worked as trackmen to clear and grade the land and to lay the tracks. Some had other duties as station helpers, brakemen, firemen, and engineers. They were seen as "cheap slave labor", not as people or human beings. Yet they were found to be reliable and they were the labor force that kept the South's railway lines in working order. Their services were needed when the able-bodied young white men were called to fight in the War Between the States (or the Civil War). Without their services the railroad lines would have collapsed.

Many Blacks continued to work for the railroad after the War Between the States. They faced actions they considered harassing, retaliatory, and discriminatory from both employer and co-workers. Intimidation of various kinds affected them, and they suffered in silence. I asked why they had let this go on for so long and they said that they didn't think it would do them any good to fight this kind of treatment. They feared losing jobs many of them had held for fifteen to twenty-odd years. If they voiced complaints, these complaints almost always caused some kind of retaliation.

At first I thought they were weak and had no spirit to stand up for themselves, but then I began to realize how they were subjected to harassment and retaliation. I heard some of them being called "boy" instead of by their names. They were ridiculed and sometimes made the butt of jokes. These men had gone to work for the railroad as track persons in the late 1960s and early 1970s. The tools used by the trackmen, such as the maul, pick axe, sledge hammer, shovel, claw bars, and bar levers required them to have strength, stamina, agility, and a high level of concentration. Their work was hard and their hours were long. For many years they were caught up in a struggle for workplace rights while being kept at the lowest work status — as track persons.

Were the racial tensions within the working force reduced? I don't think so. Most of the management and the majority of the white track persons were from this area as were the black track persons. They came from many of the small towns and cities in Missouri, Arkansas, Tennessee, Alabama, and Mississippi where The Company had rail lines, and they brought with them the kinds of attitudes and views that were present in these locations.

From my point of view management had to be aware of the manner in which the black workers were treated, but there were never any sessions on race relations or diversity in this work setting. The black track persons only wanted to be treated with respect and to be valued as individuals who were making a definite contribution to The Company. The track person may be at the lowest work level, but without them The Company can't function in terms of keeping the trains running to move the goods and providing services.

I learned that these men were not taking advantage of the resources I had learned to use. After some of these men saw what I was doing they also started to use these resources — to file grievances, to get additional health care coverage, check their benefits and retirement packages, and to change the way in which their vacation time was assigned.

My Ordeal After Filing Charges

I had been filing grievances through the Union about unfair treatment and incidents of discrimination for some time, but The Company denied all of my grievances, and working conditions remained the same. One day I decided to go to the Equal Employment Opportunity Commission office (EEOC) to see what actions could be taken for all of the unfair treatment I was getting.

So on October 10, 1997 I filled out a form listing the charges against my employer. I also had an interview. I had all of my information with me, including the documentation about what had occurred. I told the EEOC about the incident with my foreman, The Company having an investigation, which resulted in the foreman being suspended for ten days and required to attend a sexual harassment class, my being removed on the same day from one job I was assigned to do and placed in another job, and The Company reassigning me to work under him when he returned from the suspension. The interviewer stated that I had causes that the EEOC needed to investigate.

During the following work week The Company received the charges of harassment, including retaliation and discrimination I had filed. After the EEOC contacted The Company, Will was no longer my foreman. EEOC advised The Company that it was absolutely wrong to put a person found guilty of a charge over the person who had brought the charge — or even have them work in the same area. That was the law. Will was stripped of his position of "pride and glory", and was further embarrassed because he was found guilty of the charge. The day after the EEOC rendered this decision Will decided to transfer out of Memphis and work in another state.

From The Company's action of returning Will as my foreman, I concluded that The Company did not care about my safety. Many of the white male employees were bitter and angry, and let it be known in my presence that they wondered why The Company let a "black-assed" woman do that to Will. They said it was not right and that someone needed to do something bad to me. I had taken some action and I had to stand my ground. I planned to stand firm and to keep on fighting by any means necessary to keep my job without being harassed.

Even with Will out of the picture, The Company did not stop its efforts to get rid of me. Their next action added fuel to the fire and the pot began to boil. The Company arranged to have a young black foreman with a military background transferred in to take over our gang. He was known to be firm. He and I developed a good working relationship. He told me he had no problem with women working for the railroad. I did not give this new foreman, Paul, any reason to mistreat me so that a charge could be filed against him. The Company did not realize that the meaning of the phrase "by any means necessary" included finding ways to work with the foreman to keep this matter from becoming a "Black on Black" issue.

Paul and I were able to get along all right until The Company ordered him to tell me late one evening that I had to report to Blytheville, Arkansas the next day. I asked him how many were going. He said that I was the only one. He said he was following orders and he did not want me to be mad at him. I told him to call the person who gave him the orders and let that person know he could not send me out to work when there were three others with less seniority than I had. According to union rules, workers with less seniority had to be asked first. I told him that was one of my reasons for paying my union dues, because I knew I needed some kind of job protection. I told Paul that I needed an answer before the end of the day. Paul returned and said that all gangs were going to Blytheville, but he was not. I told Paul that I knew the rules and we all had to go by them. Paul knew that The Company was wrong but he did not want to be a part of this ordeal.

When I got to the tool house, Jason, a foreman, announced to the workers: "Anybody messing with Sheila White had better know what he is doing because that gal got her homework in order." Jason often said he did not care for Blacks but he would work with them. The gangs in our department were not too happy about going to Blytheville for several weeks. We had a choice – stay in that city for the duration of the work activity at company expense or we could use our own car to travel to and from the job site. Our work hours would be the same, 7:30 A.M. to 3:30 P.M. Because of the level of tension that could be experienced for two or more hours for the 70 mile trip each way, I chose neither to ride with anyone nor to stay at a hotel for the duration of this work activity.

The next morning I drove to Blytheville and arrived before others in my group got there. As I was getting out of my car, I was met by two young men. They looked at me and one said, "You're Sheila White from Memphis — the one who got rid of Will!" Later some of the workers in Blytheville said they were happy that he was no longer in the Tennessee yards and some said they were mad as hell. I told them I had come to work and I was not there to please anyone. I did not know these workers and they did not know me. They knew only what they had heard. Again the reputation that The Company had assigned me reached every job site before I arrived. This type of statement was voiced by railroad workers everywhere I went and worked, both in and out of town.

I was more or less a loner that day. I had put distance between me and all of the workers, including my gang. At the end of this day I used actual distance to separate myself from these work gangs by driving home alone.

After a briefing one morning, Nathan, the senior foreman in Blytheville, began to chat with me. He seemed to be an understanding person. He and I seemed to connect about the reasons for this work assignment. During the time his gang and our Memphis gang were together, there was cooperation, along with the desire to get the job done without delay.

My job performance had been evaluated and the report was good. Near the end of those "great" two weeks, we had a surprise visitor, my foreman from Memphis. I learned that Andrew was on a mission. The Company wanted to keep a check on what I was doing. He quietly told me that The Company wanted to get rid of me because I was a trouble maker. If my group was successful in getting rid of me, their reward would be a new gang truck. My group really needed a new truck.

The next morning Andrew took over the responsibility for our gang. As foreman, he wanted to assign me to ride in the truck from the tool house to the job site with Nathan, a senior foreman and his Blytheville gang. Andrew, with less seniority than Nathan, said he had something else to do. I went to Nathan to let him know that I was ordered by my foreman to ride with his gang to the job site. I learned that Andrew had given another worker an order also to ride with Nathan and the Blytheville gang. Nathan told me that he was keeping the male worker, and that I was to go back to my foreman for the day. Nathan then drove off. I was left without any way to get to the job site.

I returned to Andrew, my foreman, to give him Nathan's message. Andrew was very upset and began cursing, and then yelling that he had told me what to do and I did not do it. He told me to get in the truck while he went in the tool house. Another worker was in the truck waiting for Andrew to return. We were both wondering why it was taking him so long to come to the truck.

When Andrew returned to the truck, he said that he had called Gary, the supervisor in Memphis, to let him know what had happened. He said he was instructed to tell me to get my belongings and drive back to Memphis because I was suspended by Larry for insubordination.

The time was now 10:00 A.M. I drove the seventy miles back to Memphis, getting angrier by the mile. I went home and called the Union; I knew I had to file a grievance immediately. Two people were involved and both had been given the same orders. I was not permitted to ride with the senior foreman nor with my foreman. It was my foreman's duty to see that I got to the work site. This was one of the purposes for his having The Company truck. The one person suspended was me. I filed a grievance with the Union that charged the management with discrimination and retaliation under Title VII of the Civil Rights Act of 1964.

I went to the EEOC and filed charges against The Company. The first one on December 4, 1997 was for retaliation. The second one was on December 15, 1997 for discrimination and retaliation in relation to this suspension.

How long would I have to wait to hear about The Company's action on my situation? The Company made no immediate investigation based on my grievance. Yet The Company froze all benefits, including the pay I was due to receive for the work period in Blytheville, Arkansas.

All of this was happening right at the first of December and just before the Christmas season. What would my family do since I was no longer bringing in a paycheck? My two daughters were in college and my son was in high school. How were we going to live without a regular source of income?

Luckily, I had taken out an additional health insurance that allowed me to get medical attention. But my family had fallen below the poverty level. We had no money! I was becoming angry, bitter, and depressed.

I waited and waited and waited to be notified of The Company's investigation. I was in constant contact with my Union representative as he tried to get this matter resolved. Instead of being advised when to return to work, I received a letter in December 1997 from The Company requesting that I return all of my equipment since I had been fired. I had been told verbally that I had been suspended, but I had never received anything in writing, even on the day this action occurred. I had no intentions of returning any equipment because I was waiting for the investigation that The Company was obligated to conduct. I contacted Bill, my Union representative, at once about this letter.

His investigation showed that The Company had no case against me. I was not guilty of insubordination since I was following the orders of a senior foreman. Also according to company rules based on an agreement of understanding with the Union, I should have been allowed to remain on the job while the investigation took place. I was not supposed to lose any pay or benefits while this matter was being looked into. He had this charge removed from my record. He told me that I was a strong person to stand up against the abuse directed toward me. After being successful with this grievance he was moved elsewhere in the Union.

I was reinstated and received a telephone call advising me to return to work on January 15, 1998. I informed The Company that I would report to work on the next day after the Martin Luther King holiday. This was one day I had faithfully observed even before it became a national holiday to honor Dr. King for the civil rights work he had done. Now the railroad did not give this day as a day of leave for workers. Workers had to use a personal day or vacation time if they chose to celebrate this day. I also felt like a "Rosa Parks" in terms of being punished for standing up for my rights in the workplace.

In the meanwhile The Company was in no hurry to pay me my back wages and to reinstate my benefits. I had to wait until the second pay period in February 1998 (after the 15th) to receive my money. I was without an income – money that I had earned – for thirty-seven days. My ordeal helped me develop a great respect and appreciation for the sacrifices that Dr. King and others made for all of us to have a better world. It also helped me to see that some of the same things Dr. King worked to eliminate still exist, and still need to be fought.

My State Of Mind

I was ready to go back to work. I had hoped that there would be no more harassment by my employer. Actually nothing had changed regarding the way I was treated by my superiors. Harassment and retaliation had to be dealt with daily, and I soon began to dread going to work every morning. My participation in The Company's social affairs came to an end after I found myself to be the center of attention. Everybody attending the events wanted to see that "Sheila White", and I felt the pressure of their eyes staring at me. Whispered comments were heard and they sounded as echoes in both open and closed areas. I was very uncomfortable in the presence of family and friends of company employees. At safety meetings I was the only female track person there. The out-of-town railroad employees attending these sessions always wanted to see "that Sheila White"; some would speak and some would not. Again I would be the center of attention.

I was able to remain on the job for one and one half months before I had to get medical treatment again. Immediately my physician, Dr. Lindsey, recognized that I was trying to cope with my situation and that the medicines she was giving me would not cure the physical pain I was experiencing. I also was under a great deal of stress, along with being depressed. She recommended that I take medical leave for several months and helped me see the need for therapy. Medical leave began in March 1998.

I found a therapist, Dr. Olds, who helped me gain control of myself and my situation. She sent reports on me to my union and the union representative sent a copy of the report to The Company. She also requested extensions for medical leave as needed. This procedure was one that my union representative and I set up. We wanted to make certain that there would be no mishaps. We did not want to give The Company any reason to try to fire me. Also this would be a good way to keep the union and The Company informed about my status and the date I would be ending my sick leave.

In the meanwhile I had to keep my wits about me and concentrate on getting my health condition under control. I followed the medical advice of my doctor and took the medicines she prescribed. I maintained regular contact with my therapist and kept myself occupied. I had to stay busy and work through all of the emotional turmoil I had experienced. I had gone into a shell in order to protect myself on the job. I could feel a change in my personality.

Outside the therapist I had only three people I could talk to about what was happening to me in my work. I really had to put my life back in order and again have close contact with my family. This time was spent in different ways. I put my notes in order, had conferences with my attorney on the pending court case, read books and completed a self-study course to prepare myself for a state examination. I worked inside my house and in my yard to keep busy.

In all, I was out for about nine months, from mid-March to December 1998. This effort to mend my health was worth the time; I really did feel better and believed I would once again be able to handle going back to work.

Return To Work

January 1999 – I returned to work and met Mark, my new foreman and Gary, my new supervisor. I knew I had to work with Mark. The foreman had control over the worker's pay. He entered the number of hours of work and the rate of pay for the payroll into the computer. He gave each worker a print-out showing the hours worked and the pay for that pay period.

It was in each worker's best interest to keep up with the hours he or she worked. When the worker's record of hours he worked differed from the foreman's record, there was a formal procedure for the foreman to review and make corrections and for the workers to receive the omitted amount of money in a supplemental check. Some foremen made the corrections and the workers immediately received their money. I was told that I had to wait until the next pay period to receive this additional pay. As for Gary, he had a reputation of being the worst of worst as a foreman.

The very first day I was back at work, Gary attended the morning briefing. He said he had heard about me. He wanted me to know that I was going to do what he said and he did not care if it was different from what the rule book stated. I let him know that I would follow the rule book even if his instructions and orders were different. Right then it was obvious that we did not see "eye-to-eye" on going by the rule book. I knew that I would not knowingly or intentionally break the rules although there was evidence that rules were often broken. According to the rule book the track person or a worker was supposed to call his foreman about particular matters. Gary who was a supervisor told me that the rule for me was that I had to call him, not my foreman. Gary had stated his position toward me and this indicated that he did not care for me as a track person with the railroad and his job was to find a way to get rid of me. I did not have positive feelings for Gary, but I knew I had to work under his supervision.

Each morning he would come to the tool house for our briefings. He would shake hands with all the workers as he greeted them — except for me. Gary never shook my hand nor extended a morning greeting. His action of ignoring me was obvious to all of the workers, and this bothered me. I wanted to be respected as a human being and a person.

During roll call, he would call me "gal" rather than use my name. I corrected him by saying, "Sir, I have a name. Call me Sheila or 'Ms. White' or don't call me — period." The heat was on because he kept his eyes on me all of the time. He did not like for me to open my mouth since it seemed like I was constantly defending myself. Everybody knew that if he came to me in the wrong way, I would have a valid reply. I had to work hard to tolerate him and not become too embittered.

Many times Gary would come to the job site either before or after the lunch break and stop me from working with my gang. I wondered why I had been singled out to run particular errands. I had to drive him to Arkansas and drop him off at a job site. He would ride The Company train back to Memphis. He gave me specific instructions about where to park his personal car and where to place the key to his car. I learned that he would call my foreman at the yards to find out what time I made it back to the job site. Even though I asked him to get someone else, I had to drive him many times. I believe this was a set-up and something was being planned to trap me. I never felt comfortable with this situation. Thank goodness I never had a mishap.

Usually at safety meetings we wore our "street" clothing. All of us had done this for each monthly meeting. At the end of one meeting, our supervisor told us that we were to return to work. The two females, Sue and I, did not have work clothing in our car. We told Gary that we needed to go home to get them. Sue, a foreman, worked in and out of various job sites as a floater. Gary told Sue she did not have to return to work. I asked if I could be excused. He saw my expression when he gave his answer. He told me "NO!"

He told me that I had a certain amount of time to get my gear and clothing and return to work. When I returned with time to spare, the men in my gang were happy to see me. They told me that Gary had been standing by the tool house door with watch in hand, waiting to see if I would be late. He seemed disappointed when I returned with time to spare.

No one in the gang wanted to work with me or be around me because Gary was constantly there, checking up on me. I knew that he was looking for something so he could "write me up" and start the process for firing me. He would stop the gang truck I was riding in, just to see if I had on my seat belt. I had to keep my seat belt fastened all the time I was in that truck, even if we were not ready to leave the yards. Otherwise, he would submit a written report on me.

Gary proved to be an unusual man who took extreme measures to try to get me out. He had other workers check to see if I was late for work. I did not worry about this surveillance because I was usually the first person to report for work. If the gates were still locked, my car was the first car in line to get to the tool house.

He cut my pay by having some of my work hours left off the pay schedule. In addition he prevented me from contacting the payroll department about my pay. I had to have my foreman, Mark, forward any requests about pay and leave time to the payroll department. The other workers needing some information could call directly. I ran into difficulty in getting any information on job openings from the manpower division. Gary kept the doors shut on me and had certain departments and/or divisions declare me a nuisance. Again I filed a report with both the Union and The Company. When there was no action to remove this block, I filed a charge with the EEOC for discrimination.

When I tried to bid on jobs that had been posted, he would have the bidding process closed so I couldn't post my bid. Everything I tried to do by the rule through The Company did not work. I remembered the phrase, "by any means necessary" and I set up my own system to get the information I needed. I would arrive very early and stop at the main office where I had a staff member get the job information for me. I read the bulletin board for job positions and bid dates. I learned how to fax information and I would submit my requests before my work day was to begin.

I learned how devious and determined Gary could be. He wanted to get me off his gang and to keep two workers he liked. Now keep in mind the seniority rule; I had more seniority than these two men, so Gary cut the *whole* gang and started a new one. I bid on this gang and won a spot. Gary was very angry and he told Eddie, the foreman, to make my job as hard as possible. He wanted Eddie to spread the story that I had filed a sexual harassment charge on all of the men in my gang. Gary wanted the men to stop talking to me and file complaints against me. The grapevine was buzzing with this bit of information. I asked my foreman, Eddie, about this rumor. When he found out that I knew about this ruse, Eddie was mad as hell; this information was supposed to be kept private. I told Eddie that whoever told him that I had filed a sexual harassment complaint about my co-workers was telling him a lie and he was spreading it. I also told Eddie that whoever was putting him up to do this dirty work was having him dig a grave for himself.

But about one hour before the end of this hot and humid work day, I had another obstacle to face. Eddie told me in front of all of the co-workers that I needed to cut a rail. I would have to use the rail saw. I said to him that he had to be joking and that I was not going to cut that rail because I had not been trained to use a rail saw. He said that if I did not cut the rail I had to go home and not come back until he called me. A few minutes later he asked me if I wanted to cut the rail or go home. I said again I did not have the skills or training on the job to cut the rail; I would go home.

Now what did I do? On the way out of the Tennessee yards, I stopped by the main office to talk with my supervisor. He wasn't in, and I called another supervisor to tell him what had happened. He told me that I did the right thing and that he would hold a meeting with my foreman and me. He said for me to go home and have a nice day. I felt better. He said that the rule was that workers were to have proper training through classes or on the job training to use certain kinds of equipment. The rail saw was listed as one of them. I had not had this type of training.

The next morning I went to work. In the main office Alex, the supervisor, Eddie, my foreman and I had a conference. I expressed concerns about using the rail saw. Alex asked Eddie about his statement. Alex then told Eddie he was wrong and asked if he would have anyone else do the job without proper training. I was not suspended. I went back to work.

Out of nowhere Gary, my supervisor, appeared, stopped me from working and asked me if everything was handled properly. I said that it was handled in a well-mannered way. I did not make any further comments as I was aware of the less than amicable relationship between Gary who was white and Alex who was black. They had very different views over how the rule book was to be used.

Eddie was not pleased with Alex's decision. He kept telling everyone that I was supposed to be suspended. Well, it did not happen. I had gone by the rules, but it appeared that my gang would suffer again.

At the safety meeting we learned that our building was to be remodeled. I asked if a restroom for women was included. Women who visited our department also needed a decent restroom. I mentioned that other departments in buildings had such facilities for women. Gary looked at me and said, "Sheila, I would get you a 'johnny' on the spot – pink or purple, your choice." Everyone looked at me because they knew I was going to respond to that statement. I told him that his reply was not funny and in a very sarcastic way I told him that he could come up with something better than that. The bottom line was that a restroom was needed for women who came to visit in this building.

After this safety meeting I did not feel well and I arranged for a doctor's appointment for the next day. Dr. Lindsey, my medical doctor, was alarmed when she heard how I was feeling. Her examination found that my blood pressure was extremely high and I would need to take medication to regulate it. I had never had any difficulty like this before. She ordered me to take several days off work and then return to see her.

Upon my return to Dr. Lindsey, she found that my condition had not improved. She again suggested that I apply for a leave of absence for medical reasons. This leave was granted and I again sought services of a therapist to help me deal with traumatic situations around work and to get control of myself again. I found a good therapist who worked closely with me for several months in 1998 and helped me work through many problems. Dr. Grant willingly used the procedure the union representative, Bill, and I had worked out to keep The Company informed about my health status and to request leave extensions as needed. Without the work related health insurance policy I had taken out, I would not have been able to take extended leave.

Gary, my supervisor, sent me a letter to inform me that The Company was firing me as of December 7, 1998 because The Company had not received medical reports from my doctor in a timely manner. With the help of Dr. Grant and union representative Bill, this matter was cleared up by April 1999. I waited for weeks to hear from The Company about the date I would report for work. When I called The Company, I was given the run-around that there were no jobs available, and again I had to use a division within The Company called Manpower Services to find positions that were open in the surrounding areas.

On another occasion in late April 2000, I had to take time off because of severe pain in my hands. The tests and examinations I had in February and April confirmed that I was suffering from carpal tunnel syndrome. These medical reports were sent to my company, but The Company said that my medical reports and a request for extension until the middle of June 2000 had never been received. The Company advised me that they were terminating my employment. Again I had to get this straightened out through the Union and my doctor, who confirmed that this information had been sent. This matter was finally cleared up on September 9, 2000.

The Company sent me letters about my reinstatement and about what I needed to do to demonstrate I was able to work. There were no jobs available, but when one became available, I had to (1) appear before company medical personnel to be certified as physically fit to return to work, (2) take certain qualifying tests, both psychological and physical, before I could return, and (3) start as a new hire when I returned. This was not right and I used the services of the union again to get this matter worked out. The Company apologized for sending such a letter.

On August 28, 2000 my suit containing the charges of harassment, including sexual harassment, retaliation, and discrimination against The Company was set for hearing in the District Federal Court. This case was decided on September 5, 2000. A judgment was entered against The Company and I was awarded $43,500.00, plus medical fees and attorney fees.

The Company still had no job offer for me. In the meanwhile I was at home and I could call the manpower division to inquire about job openings in the Tennessee yards and in other locations. The Maintenance of Way Department had an opening in Chicago, Illinois, and I went there to work in September, 2000. Sure enough, I had to take the entry test that all new hires had to take, but I kept my seniority status.

The work situation in Chicago was great. I did not experience any harassing, humiliating, or retaliatory actions at all. My work gang was made up of Hispanic men, but there was no racial tension. We worked well together to get work assignments completed. Again, I was the only woman in the department. I found that the duties of the track person were not different from what I had in Memphis, Tennessee, but there was one great difference; the workers in Chicago had machines and equipment that made the heavy work activity seem lighter. We worked our eight hour shift and then went home. For derailments there was a special crew for call-outs, so I didn't have to work those assignments.

Positive things were beginning to happen. I had money to take care of my responsibilities, but I had to arrange for living away from home and for providing for my family in Memphis. This was not easy, but I managed to get home every weekend. This brighter picture soon dimmed however, when layoffs due to the cold weather occurred.

I returned to Memphis and to the Tennessee yards before the end of 2000 to a position I secured. All hell broke lose in the Tennessee yards when the management learned that with my seniority I had bumped someone they had wanted to remain in that position. Gary, my supervisor, arranged to have me work mostly out of the yards beginning early in 2001. The job sites included New Albany, Mineral Wells, and Olive Branch, Mississippi, Portageville, Sikeston, and Cape Girardeau, Missouri, and Marion, Wilson, Marie, Joiner, Turrell, and Lepanto, Arkansas. Sometimes members of my gang worked at these sites. Other times I worked with the track persons assigned to these work sites.

There were periods of time during late 2001 and early 2002 that I worked with my gang in the yards. We did repair work, laid new rails, constructed rail crossings, and handled derailment work. My supervisor, Gary, told me around 3:00 P.M. on a Friday that I had to report to a job site in Birmingham, Alabama the next work day (Monday, 7:00 A.M.). I would be working with a rail gang to lay rails. He said that I would have to make hotel arrangements at my expense for staying in Birmingham until this work was completed.

When I reported, the new supervisor, Barry, was waiting for me to arrive at the job site. I was told that I would be working on a gang that replaced rail from state to state. Barry talked quite frankly to me on a one-on-one basis. He said there seemed to be a problem between me and a Memphis supervisor. I said, "Sir, I do not have a problem. They may have a problem with me. I wish to work without any harassment. Is that fair, or not?" He replied, "Yes. They want me to get rid of you here. I don't know you, just about you. You seem to be a good person." I appreciated his comments.

Barry asked whether my Memphis foreman had made arrangements for a hotel room at company expense for me. I told him that this had not been done. He arranged for me to have a hotel room for the week and instructed me on how to reserve a room for every week I had to work on this job site. He told me that this was company policy. Workers were to be responsible only for their food. As I thought about what Barry said, I remembered that Gary never gave me any information on how to arrange hotel reservations when I had to work at locations away from the yards for a number of weeks. I could not afford to pay out of my pocket for this kind of expense. So I would drive to and from the work site each day, even if the distance was over fifty miles one way.

At the hotel I shared a room with one white female worker, Sally, from Kansas City. The company rule was for two people of the same sex to share a room. Sally and I were able to get along well, but we did different jobs. There were several white female workers who operated or serviced machines. Their type of work was less strenuous than the work of the track persons. I did not mind that my job was harder than hers but it bothered the men during the month and a half we worked together. Some spoke to Barry the supervisor, about how some of the men were running over each other to drive Sally to a restroom in town. We were working in an open field. Later when I had to use the restroom, I had to walk several miles to get to the truck, drive to the restroom location and then return to the job site.

When these men learned about what I had to do, all hell broke lose. They told the foreman, Carson, that he had better treat me like they treated Sally. They did not want to see me walk that long distance to the truck. Tension began to build at this railroad site but the men began to look out for my welfare. They were stating that I was a woman just like Sally and I was to be treated fairly. They also saw the difference in the kinds of work Sally and I were doing. Sally was filling in – operating the machines while the men were taking breaks. The men got the attention of Supervisor Barry. Now Barry wanted me to return to Memphis.

At Friday morning briefings he would say, "Sheila, you can go back to Memphis to work." I told him that I was not going back since there were no openings. The men got tired of hearing him making this statement and asked him to stop. One day a worker with a very deep and powerful voice told Barry that Sheila had said she was not going back. Barry did not make this statement again.

The Countdown

I needed to be closer to home; the not so pleasant work environment had begun to affect my health, and I needed to see my doctor in Memphis. Since I was stationed in Birmingham, I had two options. The first one was to leave the work site early, drive 260 plus miles to Memphis, get the medical attention, and then drive back to the work site the next day. My second option was to return to Memphis at the end of the work day, take the next day off to get the needed medical attention, and return to the job site the next work day. I chose second option.

After my doctor's visit, I decided to check on what positions were available in the yards. I found a position and bid on it based on my seniority. I was in a better frame of mind when I returned to Birmingham to resume my work there. I knew I would return to the Tennessee yards in Memphis as soon as the position I bid on became available.

My return was not anticipated by The Company. Upon my return I was assigned to a work gang headed by Carter. I had worked with his group of track persons before. I was readily accepted by them. My new supervisor was Carson.

At a safety meeting there was a discussion about the trackman position. The Company was setting up a new position of machine operator and was abolishing the position of trackman. All workers would have to meet the qualifications of a machine operator. All who did not meet the qualifications would have to take the required training to get a job as a machine operator. We learned also that all of the trackman gangs would be furloughed. In order to get work as track persons we would have to seek job openings outside of Memphis and bid on these positions. Seniority again was a key factor.

Management would begin soon to furlough the trackmen and fill the new positions of machine operator. The reason for this action was obvious for several reasons. The Company wanted to get me out of the yards and if I wanted to work as a track person I would have to find work elsewhere. The men in my gang had machine operator skills which they had developed during their long years of work experience and could fill these positions immediately.

About two weeks after this safety meeting I went to see my doctor because I was having some serious problems. I had shooting and throbbing pain in my wrists and hands. I walked the floor practically all night because I could not sleep. I lost my appetite and began to lose weight very fast, and my medications were not helping.

My doctor suggested that I take some time off and I again received medical leave. While I was on leave, I received notice that my position as trackman had been abolished. I was angry about what was happening to me. I decided to find out what was taking place at The Company. I learned that the newly created position of machine operator in the Tennessee yards was actually the trackman position, same duties, but with a new name. Seven new workers had been hired. I had more seniority than any of the seven newly hired employees. I submitted a bid, based on my seniority, on one of these positions.

I believed that The Company had cut off my job in the yards in the wrong way. Now I used the services of my union representative and my attorney to fight The Company on this action. Surely enough, my position as trackman was restored. I went back to work after my leave was up.

In September 2002, all signs were indicating that I had to give up this kind of work. The results of the various tests

Dr. Lindsey had scheduled in 2000, 2001 and 2002 indicated a progression of serious health problems. The x-rays and Magnetic Resonance Imaging (MRI) examinations revealed that I had three ruptured discs and carpal tunnel injury in both hands. I had developed high blood pressure and my blood pressure was in the danger zone. In addition to a high level of stress, I was in a depressed state. Dr. West provided a second opinion through tests, examinations, X-rays, and MRI screenings. His findings confirmed that I had carpal tunnel syndrome in both wrists and ruptured discs. Surgery would be my only option.

Medical leave became necessary again. On October 10, 2002 I applied for medical leave. It was granted and I left the job at the Tennessee yards. It was time now for me to get my health back in shape and return to work. Days passed into weeks; then weeks became months and months turned into almost five years. Some days were good; some were fair; and others were terrible as I wrestled with appointments and tests to find out what surgeries I would need and when they would be performed.

Also during this time I did not have to face any harassment, humiliation, or retaliation each day as I did while working, but on the other hand I still had to make sure that my medical reports were received by The Company in a timely fashion. This activity was both tedious and time consuming. I learned how to select personnel in the doctors' offices and at the union who would get my paperwork in when it was due. I also learned to double-check to see if the reports were received by The Company. In addition I always requested and received a copy of the information that was submitted to put in my personal files.

From October 2002 to January 2003 I had more tests and examinations. Between 2003 and 2004 I had surgery on both hands for carpal tunnel syndrome and surgery twice for the ruptured discs. Progress was slow and finally Dr. West told me that I would have to learn how to manage the pain. For the pain in my foot, he found that I had sustained a hairline fracture although I had always worn steel-toe safety shoes on the job. He believed that in time this fracture would heal on its own. I remained in therapy throughout this period of time.

Since I was still on sick leave The Company received the medical and progress reports from all of my doctors. The last report from Dr. West in early 2005 stated that I would not be able to do the work of a track person.; I would need to do lighter work.

The Company held a hearing later in 2005 with Attorney Michaels, my legal representative, Dr. West, the surgeon, and me. In the final analysis The Company representatives stated that The Company's decision was not to return me to work as a track person. The Company declared me to be medically disabled for work as a track person. The company had no other position for me as a track person or in any other capacity. I went on medical disability.

While I was involved with this matter with the Company, I learned that some of my co-workers with 20 to 30 years of railroad service were taking some bold steps. They felt empowered to explore medical problems that were job related. They had some of the same job related problems that I had, but they referred to them as "wear and tear" injury. They had suffered for many years with little or no relief from the medical attention they'd been receiving, and I really felt good about their action to get quality medical help and to take medical leave. They would no longer suffer in silence.

It seems that I left the impression that a person could be strong, stand up for one's rights, and do something about their situation. These men had said, "If Sheila can do something about her job injury, we can too." The Company lost the services of many experienced trackmen.

Saving Myself, the Railroad, and Everyone Else

I was confident that I could wait patiently for the court action against the railroad to play out. Little did I realize that glitches could or would occur in the way this matter would make its course through the court system. Sometimes I felt like I was on a bumpy roller coaster ride, going up and down, but mostly down.

My first ride on this roller coaster was in the United States District Court, Western Division, in Tennessee. My case was set to be heard on August 28, 2000 in Memphis by a federal judge who had the reputation of being very stern and firm. When he spoke, every person in his courtroom listened. The jury for my case was made up of five men and four women. The males were business executives, airplane pilots and a cleaning service driver. The women were secretaries, a day care worker and a retiree. In hindsight these people were not my peers – in terms of the kind of work I did. The trial began on August 28, 2000. For three days testimony was given. The Court was recessed for the Labor Day holiday. When it reconvened, the jurors heard some additional testimony and then began their deliberations. On September 5, 2000 the jurors found my company guilty of retaliation and awarded me a judgment of $43,500.00 plus medical fees and attorney fees. I felt devastated when the jurors did not include the sexual harassment charge.

Another down period took place when I was told that The Company planned to appeal the decision of the jury, the judgment and payment of attorney fees. I had heard The Company's representatives after the court hearing say over and over that I should never have won that decision. The Company had acted within the law. They would push The Company to appeal this court decision. The Company went to the Sixth District Court of Appeals in Cincinnati, Ohio by filing a motion for judgment as a matter of law on a retaliation claim.

For months I waited for The Company's appeal to be set for a hearing by the Sixth District Court of Appeals in Cincinnati. Now I could see that much more was involved than the judgment and fees. The retaliation charge was hurting The Company. It was fighting for the right to continue as it was doing under its understanding of how the law (Title VII) worked.

Their appeal was heard on June 11, 2003 by a three judge panel. I really believed that the justices would find that The Company was at fault. Instead this panel of judges, in a 2-1 decision, ruled in favor of The Company. The decision meant that The Company's actions toward me did not violate Title VII in regard to the retaliation provisions.

When attorneys Adair and Evins told me about the decision I was very, very upset. I felt like I had been hit by a bomb. My attorneys told me not to give up. I had to deal with this low point while they appealed the three-judge decision. Months passed before they were successful in getting an en banc hearing where the full court would hear the case and make a decision. The Court (en banc) denied The Company's motion and found that the adverse employment actions were within the meaning of the retaliation provisions in Title VII.

When my attorneys, Adair and Evins, called me early on April 25, 2004 I was so happy to hear that the Appeals Court had ruled in my favor. This news made my day!

I asked what the next step would be. My attorney laughed and said, "Sheila, you know The Company is going to appeal that decision. It will ask the Appeals Court to rehear the case." I asked what would be the next step if the Appeals Court turned down The Company's request. He said, "We will *all* go to the Supreme Court. So get ready."

Sure enough, The Company decided to appeal the decision of April 24, 2005 and asked the Appeals Court for a rehearing. Again I was on edge as I waited for action again in the Court of Appeals in Cincinnati. On August 26, 2005 the court refused to rehear the case. To the highest court in our country, The Company went in search of a decision in its favor. The Company attorneys filed their request on July 13, 2005. They went through the procedure to have the right to file a petition. With everything in place, they had their petition ready for filing on December 5, 2005. Later I would learn that the case was scheduled for arguments in April 2006. This hearing before the Supreme Court would be based one point or question: This was another low period for me because I had waited so long for a favorable decision. I had to deal with my feelings while I waited.

Attorneys Adair and Evins told me the wait for some action at the Supreme Court level was coming to an end. A date for the arguments had been set. They worked untiringly to gather needed information and they had me involved in reviewing some of the materials. They also received help from many professional groups that had an interest in a case like this one. Publicity about this case brought national attention about the right to work and what had happened to me through my company. Yet strange as it may seem this matter did not receive much attention in my home town. Friends and family kept me posted on views being expressed elsewhere about how the Supreme Court would deal with retaliation in relation to Title VII.

Attorneys Adair and Evins repeatedly told me that they were confident that they would be victorious. They wanted me to attend this hearing when they presented their argument. The date for this momentous occasion finally arrived. It was April 17, 2006.

I was tingling with excitement because I would be allowed to attend this hearing. The morning of the hearing was a gloomy gray and wet day filled with a thunderstorm. I tried to be cheerful and upbeat although the weather was horrible. I anxiously waited for the screening process to end so I could enter the courtroom. Security was very heavy. I could not take my umbrella in with me. The Marshall told me to rent a locker and place it there.

My case which Burlington Northern had appealed was the second one to be heard. The courtroom was filled with people for that case and for mine. The first case was completed within the allotted time period. Very few people left the courtroom. So it appeared that most of the spectators had come for my case.

Just being present during the arguments made before the nine justices of the Supreme Court was one of the highest points in this ordeal. This group – Justices Samuel A. Alito, Jr., Stephen G. Breyer, Ruth Bader Ginsburg, Anthony M. Kennedy, John G. Roberts, Jr., Antonin Scalia, David H. Souter, John Paul Stevens, and Clarence Thomas – presented an impressive picture. I sat with a large group of law students. My attorney purposefully came over with a feather in his hand and said, "Sheila, this is for you." When he did that, everybody knew that "Sheila White" was in the house. These students were so excited to know who I was.

Everyone sat and listened intently through the hearing, which lasted longer than the allotted time. I heard each justice ask questions. I listened carefully to the answers each attorney gave and to the statements the justices made. I was impressed with Justice Ginsburg, Justice Breyer and Justice Scalia because they were asking the attorneys for Burlington Northern most of the questions. The questions were direct and focused on the issue at hand. Yet all of the justices seemed genuinely interested in the case and the law that was involved. I believed that the decision would be favorable to us. I also knew that the outcome in this case, if in my favor, would be powerful enough to make The Company change its way of handling harassment, retaliation, and discrimination charges. The Company would be saved from wrecking itself.

When the arguments were over and we had vacated the courtroom, many people came over to talk to me. They felt like I did – the decision would be in my favor. As I went outside the Supreme Court building, many reporters were standing on the steps, waiting for me. I had not prepared myself for such an event, but I stood there with my attorneys and answered a series of questions for the media representatives. As I went down the steps, I replayed that impulsive action I took with my umbrella before I went into the courtroom; I had discarded it too hastily! The wind was blowing the rain, which was suddenly coming down very hard on all of us. Everyone raced for cover. I ran to catch a taxi to escape from the media. I was drenched, but never mind — this was my day. I felt good. I felt relieved. I felt vindicated.

The wait for a decision of the justices was not easy. Every day we wanted to know what the justices were thinking. My attorneys, my family, and my friends all cautioned me to be patient. My attorneys told me over and over that the justices would make their ruling just before end of their 2005-2006 court calendar. Now this really happened.

On the morning of June 22, 2006 Attorney Adair called. He was so excited that he was yelling, *"We won! We won! Do you hear me? We won the Supreme Court decision 9-0. You set a precedent!"* This was one time in my life that I felt joy and relief from all the tension that had built up over a nine year period.

The decision of the Supreme Court in my case would create one single national rule to tell what retaliation is. This would make it easier for workers to sue if their employers retaliated against them for complaining about discrimination or sexual harassment, and it would make it much easier for companies to know how they should treat their people. As a result of the unanimous decision, The Company can no longer do to workers what it did to me and get away with it. I truly feel that this ruling stopped The Company from experiencing one of their greatest train wrecks ever. The rippling effect of this ruling will touch all employers and will open the way for employees, especially women, to seek redress for harassment, discrimination, and retaliation in the workplace.

This decision vindicated me. No one can take away this sense of accomplishment and feeling of satisfaction.

When I hear that whistle blow, I can say, "Just blow on!" If the train jumps the track, it won't be me who catches hell. I don't have to help put it back on track. I am already on track and moving ahead with full steam.

Special Thanks To...

My husband, Andrew Parrish
for helping and supporting me.

Barbara McKissack Chalmers
for getting me to stay the course.

My parents,
Dr. Leon Patrick Davis & Ruby Taylor Davis
who encouraged me to write this book.

And all family and friends
who wondered and waited for me to finish it.

Commentary

  I wrote this book, based on personal experiences, to show what happened to me, a woman in a male dominated workplace. I hope and pray that no other working women would have to endure such conditions.

  I would like for this book to be a lifter for all working women in the workplace. To them, I would say:

"Women, Shake the Foundation!"

Resources

EEOC. For information about harassment, discrimination and retaliation in the workplace, e-mail info@ask.eeoc.gov (Please include your zip code and/or city and state so that your e-mail will be sent to the appropriate office).
You can also visit http://www.eeoc.gov or write:

> U.S. Equal Employment Opportunity Commission
> 1801 L Street NW
> Washington, D.C. 20507

EEOC's customer service representatives are available to assist you in more than 150 languages between 8:00 a.m. and 8:00 p.m. EST. An automated system with answers to frequently asked questions is available on a 24-hour basis. (800) 669-4000 TTY: (202) 663-4494

Resources (Cont.)

Arnesen, Eric. (2001) Brotherhood of Color: Black Railroad Workers and the Struggle for Equality. Harvard University Press. Retrieved from:
http://www.hup.harvard.edu/catalog/ARNBRO.html

Chat. Wikipedia. Retrieved from:
http://en.wikipedia.org/wiki/Chat

Hoover's Profile. Burlington Northern and Santa Fe Corporation. Retrieved from:
http://www.answers.com/topic/burlington-northern

Jobs4u Career Database. Rail Track Maintenance Worker. Transport and Logistics. Retrieved from:
http://www.connexions-direct.com/jobs4u

Occupational Diseases. Creosote. Retrieved from:
http://www.occupationaldiseaseinfo.com

Title VII of the Civil Rights Act of 1964. Labor Issues.

Retrieved from http://labor.about.com

Wilson, Arkansas. Profile. Retrieved from:
http://www.encyclopediaofarkansas.net

LaVergne, TN USA
22 April 2010
180143LV00004B/33/A